Charly's Piano

by Calogero (Charly) Chiarelli

Charly's Piano

Charly's Piano is a story by Charly Chiarelli about his experiences working at the Clarke Institute of Psychiatry in Toronto in the early 1970s, staged as Artword Theatre's Christmas production for 2017. Based on true events, the play tells how Charly the hippie organized a Variety Show with patients, nurses and doctors to raise money to buy a piano for the eleventh floor. Funny and touching, Charly's Piano evokes the spirit of a magical time in downtown Toronto.

Calogero (Charly) Chiarelli was born in Racalmuto, Sicily and raised in a Hamilton neighborhood in the industrial North End. One of Canada's premier storytellers, he is widely known for one-person plays, *Cu'Fu?*, *Mangiacake*, and *Sunamabeach*, directed by Ronald Weihs and designed by Judith Sandiford.

Filmed performances of *Cu'Fu* and *Mangiacake*, directed by Gemini Award winner Denis Beauchamp, were aired frequently on Bravo Television. As a jazz and blues harmonica player, Chiarelli has contributed to recordings and live performances as well as creating his own musical works. He has written a libretto for an oratorio called *The Birds Beyond*, with music composed by Juno Award winner John Burge, performed by the Kingston Symphony and the Thunder Bay Symphony Orchestra. Charly has also created children's works entitled *Ho Ho Hum* and *Once Upon a Pizzeria*. In 2003, he was inducted into the McMaster University Alumni Hall of Fame. In 2012, he debuted as a member of the Artword Theatre Ensemble in Artword's production *of James Street*, remounted in 2014 and 2015. He created the role of Ebenezu Scroogi (Ebenezer Scrooge) in the Artword Theatre's production of *Scroogissimo* in 2013, remounted in 2014 and 2016. He has recently completed a feature film, *Antonio's Lemon Grove*, as co-writer and leading actor.

Artword Theatre is the creation of Judith Sandiford (Managing Director) and Ronald Weihs (Artistic Director). They operated a highly successful theatre in downtown Toronto for twelve years. In 2008, they moved to Hamilton, where they operate **Artword Artbar**, a popular live-music and performance venue in the James Street North arts district, and continue to produce, write and direct original Canadian theatre.

Charly's Piano

by Charly Chiarelli and Ronald Weihs

Artword Press
Hamilton Ontario, 2017

First published in 2017 by Artword Press
166 Prospect Street South, Hamilton, Ontario.

Photos courtesy of Calogero Chiarelli

ISBN:

Charly's Piano

by Charly Chiarelli and Ronald Weihs

Charly's Piano was produced by Artword Theatre, 15 Colbourne Street, Hamilton, Ontario, December 7 - 16, 2017.

ACTOR/STORYTELLER:
Calogero (Charly) Chiarelli

DIRECTOR:
Ronald Weihs

PRODUCER:
Judith Sandiford

DESIGN AND STAGE MANAGEMENT:
Judith Sandiford

MUSIC:
Calogero (Charly) Chiarelli
Ronald Weihs

Preface

Charly Chiarelli was born Calogero Chiarelli in Sicily. His family immigrated to Hamilton when he was still an infant. He grew up in Hamilton's industrial North End, a district that was home in the 1950s to 10,000 Sicilians, almost all from a single town, Racalmuto. No wonder that Hamilton is twinned with Racalmuto, and that a stretch of Murray Street has been renamed "Corso Racalmuto".

Charly took a Masters of Social Work, and became a Mental Health and Addictions Counsellor. But he has had a parallel life as a storyteller, musician, actor and writer. A virtuoso on the harmonica (chromatic and diatonic), he is a master of jazz, blues, and lovely Sicilian folk tunes.

In the 1970s, while sitting in with a blues band in Toronto's Kensington Market, he met Dan Yashinsky, who was pioneering the art of storytelling in Canada. He joined the group who founded *1001 Nights of Storytelling*, a weekly gathering that has never missed a Friday since it began in 1979.

In 1995, Dan Yashinsky co-produced the *Festival of the Human Voice* with Artword Theatre. He persuaded Charly that he should take the stories he had been telling informally, about his family and growing up Sicilian in Hamilton, and shape them into a performance. The was the start of *Cu'Fu? (Who Did It?): Stories of a Sicilian Family*. *Cu'Fu?*, expanded into a two-act play with the help of director Ronald Weihs and designer Judith Sandiford, was a hit from the start. It has toured across Canada and in Europe, and was made into a film for Bravo Television by UBWired Productions, directed by Denis Beauchamp.

Cu'Fu? was followed by more plays about Charly's life as a Sicilian-Canadian. The next was *Mangiacake*, about how Charly ran for student council president of Westdale Collegiate with the slogan "Put a Wop on Top"— and won. And how he went to Sicily to find his roots. The Artword production became the basis of two more Bravo films, *Mangiacake* and *Brutta Figura*.

Artword Theatre moved to Hamilton in 2007, and in 2008 the series became a trilogy. *Sunamabeach* told the story of Charly's return to Hamilton, after 20 years in Kingston, to take the ultimate "bona jobba", Mental Health and Addictions Consultant for the entire Hamilton region.

Charly's Piano, the latest in the series, goes back to 1972, when Charly moved to Toronto to do graduate studies at University of Toronto, and got a job as a psychiatric assistant with the Clarke Institute of Psychiatry. That's when he decided that the Clarke needed a piano, and organized a fundraiser, with performances by patients, nurses and doctors.

Charly's Piano, like the other Charly plays, has been developed in collaboration with director Ronald Weihs, and designer/producer Judith Sandiford of Artword Theatre. It was Judith who first urged that the 45-minute prototype of *Cu'Fu?* should be expanded into a full-length production, and triggered the whole chain of events. This time, too, she played an instrumental role.

Charly was invited to tell a story as part of a festival of short works at The Pearl Company, a delightful Hamilton performance venue. Charly told a twenty-minute version of the story of the Clarke Institute and the piano.

Judith was excited by the possibilities. Ron got together with Charly, turned on a recorder, and got Charly talking... and talking. He transcribed the stories and shaped them into *Charly's Piano*. They presented a reading at Artword Artbar in May, with a full production following in December, 2017.

Foreword: The Dawn of Storytelling in Toronto

Based on outtakes from Charly's Piano.

by Charly Chiarelli

In 1969, I was at McMaster University in Hamilton. In 1970, I was at Mac for half a year, helped organize Clear Hamilton of Pollution (CHOP), and then came back to Mac for one semester, half a year. Then I travelled with my girlfriend for six months, and then I went to U of T for graduate studies in psychology. That's when the story of *Charly's Piano* begins. She and I started learning massage at the Ontario College of Massage.

We broke up. We were young. She ended up out west as a massage therapist. I just didn't bother to get the licence. It cost $500, after a year studying massage.

Later on, I joined the pickup band at the Brunswick Tavern, downstairs in the afternoons. Every week, for a year.

Everything musically worthwhile was going on upstairs. Downstairs was gritty, grotty, drunken students in the afternoon on Saturday. Downstairs, there was the midget who sang "Oklahoma" and the woman with the organ. And I joined them too.

I'd get a phone call. "Charly, can you come down?" All I did was play harp, and it was pretty packed, because it was right after a football game at Varsity stadium.

The old lady would sing and play the organ. And when the guy wasn't singing, he was shining shoes. He was the shoeshine guy, when you walked in.

After a while, I discovered Gaffer's Cafe in Kensington Market. They had a blues band intermittently, so I would show up jam with the blues band.

And during one of these jams, in the intermission, I'm standing beside this guy, who, strangely enough, looks like me—the way I looked then. I looked like a hippie, long hair, beard. And he looked the same.

It was Dan Yashinsky. We're standing beside each other, and he said, "You play a pretty good harmonica. But that's a terrible band." Then he looked around and said, "This would be a great spot for storytelling."

I said, "Storytelling?"

He said, "Yeah".

I said, "Here? In a restaurant, you're going to tell stories?" I thought, "He's a nut case." Kensington Market was full of nut cases.

Two weeks later, I go to jam at Gaffers. I walk into Gaffers, and there's no band. There's him, on a stool. Telling stories. And I thought, "How did this guy oust the band?"

And he's telling stories. And he's inviting people from the audience to tell stories. And he spotted me, and he said something about "stories are sometimes accompanied by music". He said, "We're going to have this story accompanied by harmonica." And he looked at me.

I took out my harmonica, and he told some stories, and I accompanied him.

Lo and behold, that was it for that place! It was storytelling every Friday night. It was called *1001 Nights of Storytelling*. It has not missed a Friday night. I named my daughter, Selina, after the proprietor of Gaffers, for allowing the storytelling. Her name was Selina Ma. She was from Hong Kong.

After a while, *1001 Nights of Storytelling* moved from Gaffers, because Gaffers closed down. It moved from there to this rickety old three-story walk-up.

And one night, there we were. It was storming out, and I noticed that we were just telling stories to each other. There were only about eight of us there that night. Nobody's coming to our Friday nights. We're telling stories to each other.

And the discussion went to, "Is this worth it? Is it worthwhile to continue the storytelling?" And then we heard steps on the rickety stairs.

The door opened. The wind blew the door open. You didn't have to open it. And there was this guy, in this raincoat, and what was conspicuous about him was the white cane that he had. He was from New York City. He was interested in storytelling, and he had done a little research, and found that there was storytelling in Toronto, and this was the location.

And our conclusion was that, if this guy could make it to storytelling, storytelling has to continue. And it has not missed a week to this day.

And it shaped my life.

I was attending regularly, but not as a storyteller. I was the accompanist and I helped with the chairs. I was the guy who told stories to the storytellers when they went into the Green Room.

That's what gave Dan the idea that I should put some of these North End stories together, and join the Festival of the Human Voice, at Artword Theatre on Portland Street.

And that was the start of *Cu'Fu? (Who Did It?) Stories of a Sicilian Family.*

Charly's Piano

Charly's Piano
Act I

Something About Toronto

Something 'bout Toronto
Fills me full of wonder
Something 'bout Toronto
Makes me buckle under
Was it luck that brought me
Or did I come by blunder?
Something 'bout Toronto town.

Many cultures blending,
A taste of every nation
Traffic never ending
Sports and celebration,
Chinatown and glitter
Date night at the theatre,
Something 'bout Toronto town.

CHORUS
Living a crazy wild city scene
Subways, streetcars – College and Queen
Love it, hate it – that's all right.
It's my life
My home.

Buildings posing pretty
Bay street talking money
Cafés posh and gritty
Music flows like honey
Kensington and Yorkville
Places where you just chill,
Something 'bout Toronto Town.

Something 'bout Toronto Town.

Toronto 1972

It was 1972. I'm crossing the street at Spadina and College. Across the street, I see my oldest friend, Marjan Mosetich. We grew up together in the North End of Hamilton. His house was joined to our house, and the wall was so thin we could talk to each other right through the wall.

What was he doing in Toronto?

I said, "Marjan! What the fuck are you doing here?"

He said, "I live in Toronto. I'm studying music at U of T." What are you doing here?"

I said, "I've just moved here."

He said, "It's about time."

"What do you mean, it's about time?"

He says, "I gotta go. I've got a class." And he ran off.

I guess Toronto was going to be my home. I found a place to live in the Kensington Market.

Porretta's pizzeria was on the corner of Harbord and Robert Streets. Mrs. Porretta cooked the most delicious pizza. Her husband was behind the counter looking after the customers, and the kids ran around as if the pizzeria was their rec room.

Next door to Porretta's pizzeria was a Primal Scream Therapy clinic. Mr. Porretta didn't know what to make of them.

"Charly. Dese people, dey scream alla time. Why dey scream?"

I said. "It's like this, Mr. Porretta. They have this theory. When they were babies, they didn't get enough screaming out. So, they feel like there's something locked inside that never came out when it was supposed to come out. So, they go to the clinic."

And he stops me, and he says, "But dey pay monee?"

I say, "Yes". I say, "The person who runs the screaming is a dottore. Psycologo."

"Ahhh." He said, "They scream every week? Every day?"

I say, "It's different people coming to scream at different times."

"Oh." And he says, "What do you want on your pizza?"

On another day, he says, "And the other ones down the street…"

He was talking about 3HO, Healthy, Happy, Holy. An ashram devoted to Kundalini Yoga The followers, men, women and children, dressed all in white, with white turbans. They made the first smoothies that I ever had. They had delicious open-faced sandwiches. No meat.

He said, "Charly, they come to order the pizza and in their pockets, in a little bag, they bring their own chopped-up garlic." He said, "You should see how much garlic they want to put on the pizza. And they no even Italian!"

I said, "Yeah, yeah Mr. Porretta. That culture uses a lot of garlic too."

He said, "What cultura they come from?"

I said, "Indian."

He said, "Cowboy, Indian, Geronimo?"

I said, "No, no. Indians. From India."

Mr. Poretta says, "But they all be Canadian, no?"

"Si, si, okay! Mr. Poretta, you gonna take my order?"

He went, "Oh, si, si! What do you want on your pizza?"

And I say, "Garlic".

He gives me that "*Madonna!*" Sicilian look.

The Harbord Jewish Bakery was nearby. I soon became addicted to cherry cheese cake.

Finding the Clarke

So, I thought, "Well, first and foremost, I need a job". Cherry cheese cake was an expensive addiction. So, I'm on College at Spadina, and I see this sign that says, "Clarke Institute of Psychiatry".

And I was reading *One Flew Over the Cuckoo's Nest* at the time. It was in my pocket. A great book by Ken Kesey, about a mental hospital run by this terrible Big Nurse, and a guy who liberates it.

I thought "Clarke Institute of Psychiatry. It makes sense. I'm studying psychology, and that sign says psychiatry." So, I just marched in there.

And I said, "Who do I have to talk to about a job?"

And she says, "Are you a social worker?"

I said, "No."

"Are you a nurse?"

I said, "No."

"Are you a doctor?"

I said, "No."

The lady checked out my long hair, beard. Scruffy clothes. And she said, "We do have a position called psychiatric assistant".

"Psychiatric assistant? Sounds good."

She said "The person who hires psych assistants is not here. The director of nursing hires them. She's on vacation."

I said, "Please make me an appointment for when she returns."

She looked at me a little oddly, and said "Okay. Two weeks from now. Two o'clock on Wednesday."

And so, two weeks later, I walk in. The Director of Nursing is there, and she looks at me, and she says, "Why do you have an appointment?"

I say, "I heard there's a position called psych assistant here, and I want the job. I'm reading *One Flew Over the Cuckoo's Nest*. And my father was in a psychiatric hospital for most of my life in Hamilton. And I'm studying psychology at the University of Toronto. And I just live around the corner."

And she hired me!

It was going to be a month before I start. And in the course of that month, I was invited to a stag. One of my buds in Hamilton was getting married.

I'm hitchhiking home to Hamilton for the stag. And this guy picks me up.

He's very articulate, and he has this great Edward G. Robinson voice, and looked like him. And he asks me where I'm going, and he seems to be interested.

He wasn't going to Hamilton. He says "I'll let you off at the next exit. I'm just going to the shoreline to dip my feet in the water. My kids are driving me crazy."

I say, "You might have trouble getting back to your car."

He went, "Pardon?"

I say, "That's Lake Ontario you're dipping your feet into. Your feet might dissolve."

He smiled and said, "And what do you do, young man?"

I say, "I got a job at the at the Clarke Institute of Psychiatry. I start in a month."

He says, "Oh, the Clarke". He says, "I'm familiar with the Clarke".

I say, "Do you work there or something?"

He says, "I'm very familiar with the Clarke".

And that's all he would tell me. And he let me off. And he went to dip his feet in Lake Ontario.

Something 'Bout Toronto (2)

Smoking up and grinning,
Running late for classes
Rush hour's got me spinning
Moving with the masses,
Manic moon above me
I need someone to love me,
Here in this Toronto Town

Fast food so exotic
Smoothies, blintzes, patties,
Yonge Street so chaotic
Strip joint, sugar daddies
Caribana, gay pride,
High Park for a bike ride.
Something 'bout Toronto town.

CHORUS
Living a crazy wild city scene
Subways, streetcars – College and Queen
Love it, hate it – that's all right.
It's my life
My home.

Queen's Park flexing muscle,
Bureaucratic mumbling,
Street folk on the hustle,
Midnight boozers stumbling,
Cruise to sunny beaches,
Sail to outer reaches
Something 'bout Toronto town.

Something 'bout Toronto town.

The Inn on the Clarke

On my first day, I was taught the ropes. It was evening and they were showing me around.

One patient was on continuous observation, because he was striking out and there was danger that he was suicidal. Continuous observation means they're in their room, you're in the hallway in a chair, and you just watch them.

I did my hour with him. He was agitated, talking a mile a minute. I just sat there. After an hour, a nurse took over, and I went on to other duties and patients.

When it was time for me to leave, I took the elevator downstairs. The security guard was there. He stopped me and said, "You! Sit right there!" And he locked the tempered glass door to the outdoors.

I could tell by his tone that he thought I was a patient. Now, this was my first day, but already I had learned one very important thing. I knew that the last thing I should do is deny that I'm a patient, or claim that I'm sane. So, I just sat there. And he disappeared.

I sat there calmly, reading my book, *One Flew Over the Cuckoo's Nest* for the second time. I figured the security guard had gone to get the nursing director. While I was sitting there, I heard a pounding on the locked glass door.

It was winter. The snow was coming down hard, and there was someone at the door, in his pajamas, barefoot, smoking a cigarette, and banging on the door. Making wild "open the door" gestures. It was the same patient I had been observing. And *he* knew I was staff. He's wondering, "Why is this fucking guy not letting me in?"

One reason is, I didn't have the key. And number two, those were not my instructions.

After a while, the nursing director came down, and she said, "Oh Charly! It's you." I said, "The security guy told me to sit here."

She said, "I'm so sorry Charly." She was very sympathetic.

I said, "Don't apologize to me. Apologize to that guy."

We could see the guy's lips moving: "What the fuck, let me in, you bastards!" He went out to buy cigarettes. In his pajamas.

He got let in, and he just walked past me and said, "What the fuck, what the fuck? Are you crazy or something?" That was my first day at work.

Winter Time Blues

Winter time blues
Snow in my shoes
A runny nose and tons of clothes
I've gotta use
Christmas lights are flashin'
Upon my winter time blues

Sloppy white snow
Traffic goin' slow
I dream of southern lands
Where winter winds don't blow
Christmas lights are flashing
Upon my winter time blues

Spring and summer got their troubles
Dark days in autumn too
Brush strokes from the winter winds
Paint the whole world blue

There's blues in the night sky
Blues in the deep blue
And even Santa's eyes they seem
More blue than they should be
More blue than they should be

Cold silent night
No sunshine in sight
And old Jack Frost is grinning
With them teeth that love to bite
Christmas lights are flashin'
Upon my winter time
Upon my winter time
Upon my winter time blues

The Clarke Institute was the most prestigious teaching hospital in North America. People called it The Inn on the Clarke. Only the most interesting patients were treated there. The crème de la crème. The boring chronic patients were sent "up the road". That's what we called it. "Up the road" to 999 Queen Street.

The Clarke was in the forefront of the movement away from the incarceration model in mental hospitals. You come in the front door and get on the elevator. Nobody screens you. And you go to the floor where you're going to visit or work. In my case, the eleventh floor.

Facing the elevator was the nursing station. It was all completely open. And if a patient wanted to escape, there was no gate or anything. They just had to wait and see whether somebody was watching from the nursing station. There was also an adjoining room in the nursing station, where we did rounds. We would give information to the next shift. That's called "rounds".

The word "rounds" was used in different ways. When you go around at night, making sure that everybody's asleep, you're doing "rounds". And there are "Grand Rounds", held in a large auditorium downstairs. If there was a patient that was exhibiting some interesting pathology, it would be presented to the staff.

And there were special events, where a psychiatrist from New York, for example, would give a presentation about Vampires and Schizophrenia. And the psychiatric assistants were free to go to any of the Grand Rounds. We were flies on the wall.

It was the secret of secrets that psychiatrists really did not know a whole lot about sanity and insanity. As a psych assistant, it was fascinating. It was the heyday of interesting insanity.

We were assigned to units, but we left our unit when there was an "all male staff call". They called it an "all male staff call" because the only female that showed up was the nurse with her needle.

I was starting to get a sense that I was very different from the other psych assistants. They dressed so elegantly and stylistically, and had this great way of expressing themselves.

They had zero sense of belligerence about them, the way they approached the patient, so gently.

My attitude was simple: let's immobilize this guy so the nurse can get her needle in his ass. I was well versed in Judo, Karate, and boxing. It's the background I came from.

But these kind souls, with the absolutely glorious style about them, did not have my North End Hamilton background. Some of them got hit in the face with things like ashtrays. And that scar! Poor Sean.

But I knew something about pressure points. You can cause pain most anywhere with a hard, steady pressure. My colleagues were always grappling. Three guys on the arms, two guys on the legs. Not me.

And they started to notice: why does Charly never need any help with the arm that he's pushing down? Well, it's because I'm causing this guy a lot of pain, and he's just looking at me. And they were honorable patients, very honorable. They didn't say, "You're fucking hurting me!" They just looked at me, and as they looked at me, I released the pain.

The other psych assistants were looking at me, and thinking, "What is that little guy doing, that he doesn't get whacked?" I eventually showed them what I was doing, but for now it was my job not to get hit in the face. That was my job for my whole life in Hamilton, because I hung out with people who liked to hit you in the face. So, you either establish yourself as a tough guy or you establish yourself as a clown. And I sort of did both.

Between the elevators there was an ashtray for cigarettes, filled with ashes and cigarette butts. It was about four or five days after I got there. I had gotten into the habit of just goofing around and practising my karate. I'd look around to see if anyone was looking, and if nobody was, I would kick at the ashtray, front kicks, sidekicks, roundhouse kicks, just missing.

On one of my front kicks I made contact with the ashtray, and the ashes and the butts went flying up into the air. The elevator door opened. I tried to look as innocent as I could.

And the first thing I saw was an elegant three-piece suit, and a whole bunch of very well-dressed young men surrounding him. He was the god, and I knew right away that guy was the god. It was the guy who picked me up hitchhiking. And he just said, "You!"

Somebody got off the elevator. And through ashes still floating down, I looked at this god, and through elevator doors that were almost closed, I said, "You!"

I asked around about who he was, and the Director of Nursing said, "Oh, that's Dr. Rakoff."

I said, "What's he do?"

She said, "You don't know? He runs the Clarke Institute."

I said, "Oh. Oh."

I Ponder

I've got songs to set me free
Power sometimes baffles me
Lost in grey reality
I ponder
Whether to be or not to be.

Making moves I can't explain
Dancing in the neon rain
Is my poetry insane
And I wonder
What will become of me?

And the future rises up
Like a mountain I must climb
And I shed a tear
for the life I leave behind
And I ponder
And I wonder
And I wonder
And I ponder.

Therefore I am
Therefore I am.

Colleagues

So, like I said, my colleagues, the psych assistants, were gorgeous guys. Well-groomed, well-built, handsome young men. I felt like the black sheep.

One of the nursing students said, "Would you tell Teddy that I like him?"

And I said, "Tell him yourself."

"Oh, please. Could you put in a good word for me?"

Anyway, on one particular occasion, I was going down to the underground parking lot to get my bicycle, and Teddy was getting his.

So, I said, "Teddy, you know that Elaine chick that is doing her nursing placement here?"

He said "Yeah...?"

I said, "She really likes you."

He went "Charly..."

And as we walked through the underground parking lot, he says, "I'm gay".

"Oh, ah. That's nice. That's great. That's..."

He just rolled his eyes and said, "And I live with Doug."

I went, "And you live with Doug?" Another psych assistant.

Jim? and Dave? and Bill? And Harry? Are all gay! This woman, who did the hiring, hired all gay guys to be psych assistants, except for me. I found that very interesting.

After she retired, I asked this Nursing Director about her hiring practice, and she said, "I didn't know those guys were gay when I hired them, Charly. I just liked their attitude. And they were so cute."

I asked, "Why did you hire me?"

And she said, "You're cute. But I don't really remember about the rest of my thinking. You were just strange, and I thought you might fit in."

I started hanging out with all these interesting gay guys. They knew how to throw a party. One time they rented a bus and we dropped acid and we went to the Toronto Zoo.

Another time, it was Doug's birthday, they rented a movie theater after hours, Cinema Lumiere on College Street. They screened Fellini's *Clowns* with no sound, and the sound system blared the rock and roll music of the time. Led Zeppelin, whatever. And people were dancing on the stage. You saw their tiny silhouettes as the movie played *Clowns*, with subtitles.

And we were smoking up in the theatre and drinking booze, celebrating the birthday. Free popcorn and free ice cream. They organized that kind of a party.

My kind of people. My colleagues and new friends. I was a long way from Hamilton. What was already outrageous about me... became more outrageous.

Finding the Blues

After my shift, I'd go home to my apartment on Robert Street. It was a two-storey house with an attic, owned by the Greek people on the first floor. Portuguese people rented the second floor, and I could never take a bath, because there was codfish in the bathtub. Bacalao. Getting soaked all the time. So, I had to take my showers at the Karate Club.

I lived in the attic. They got upset because too many women were coming to visit me. They weren't all lovers, by any means. Most of them were friends, and some were just invited over for a toke or some wine.

There was no door to the attic. So, I found this enormous, big, thick rug in the garbage. I put it on my shoulder and rode it home on my bicycle. I hung it like the Gypsies do. Now I had some privacy from my Greek landlady.

Of all my activities, the foremost was music. I learned that the harmonica was an instrument and not a toy. I'd been playing harmonica since I was a kid, but I didn't really know what it could do.

That is, until I moved to Toronto and started listening to Ryerson Radio Blues on Saturday afternoons. The announcer would say, "That was Sonny Boy Williamson on harmonica". I went, "Harmonica?" Sometimes I thought it was a violin. Or a lead guitar. Or a saxophone.

I decided I wanted to learn to play the blues harmonica. But nothing I did sounded like the blues harmonica.

One patient, Beatrice, will forever be in my heart. Her psychosis was the magic of cats. Her two Siamese cats taught her how to read minds.

She was ultra-sensitive. She said that I wasn't made of matter like the rest of them, just spirit. She said she knew, because she too was made of only spirit. As I sat in her room, she said she heard me playing harmonica in the TV room, and would I play for her? I played "Over the Rainbow."

She stopped me. She told me she had never played one, but could she try it? And she played:

The Magic of Cats

The magic of cats, cats, cats.
The magic of cats, cats, cats.

A world full of rats, rats, rats.
A world full of rats, rats, rats.

Lost in the blues, blues, blues.
I am your muse, muse, muse.

I said, "Damn it, Beatrice. I've been trying so hard to play blues like that, and I can't find it."

And she says, "Don't try to find the blues. The blues will find you."

There was this other patient, whose name was Phillip. He was brilliant. He was into astronomy, physics, just brilliant. Psychotic as hell, but just... a peace-loving young man.

I really liked this guy. And I knew that the resident who was his doctor didn't understand him at all. She didn't understand the relationship between sanity and insanity and Canadian culture. She had recently arrived from India. She didn't understand the hippie movement that had swept across Toronto.

I was doing continuous observation with this guy, because they thought he was self-destructive. And I got to sit in a chair, read a book, have a conversation, get to know him.

At one point, he said, "Charly, why are you sitting there, watching me all the time? You don't have to watch me. I'm not going to kill myself. I haven't got the guts to commit suicide. And with my fucking luck, I'll live to be 93."

And at that moment, the blues found me. He was my inspiration for my first blues song. I jotted down the lines in my book.

I'm crawlin' in the gutter, crying constantly
With my fucking luck, I'll live to be 93.

And I got it. That's the first blues song I ever wrote. And I understood the blues harmonica from it.

Down and Dirty Blues

The world is crashing down
upon my weary head.
My mind is mashed potatoes
and my eyes are red.

Got them blues, got them blues...
Got them blues, got them blues...
Them down and dirty blues
Chased me from my mama's womb.

Crawlin' in the gutter
Crying constantly
With my fucking luck
I'll live to be 93,

Got them blues, got them blues
Got them blues, got them blues
Down and dirty blues
Went and chased me from my mama's womb.

Blind when I'm drunk
Lost when I'm stoned
Die slow when I'm straight
Listen to me moan.

Got them blues, got them blues
Got them blues, got them blues
Down and dirty blues
Chased me from my mama's...

Down and dirty blues
Chased me from my mama's...
Down and dirty blues
Chased me from my mama's womb.

That patient who gave me my first blues song, well... Nobody really got a sense of who he was, but I was really getting it. His psychiatrists weren't getting it, because he wasn't divulging.

He was overmedicated. He didn't need continuous observation. He wasn't suicidal. They were all wrong about that.

So, I borrowed the reel-to-reel tape recorder. It's a big monster. I set it up and I talked to him for two and a half hours. Who was he? Where was he from? Up until then, he wouldn't divulge anything about himself. I found out he was from a wealthy family out west.

I went to Dr. Persaud, the head of the unit, and I said, "I spoke with Phillip, had a session with him, and I thought that you should hear this recording, maybe with the resident." I gave him the tape.

They contacted the family. They came from out west. He was discharged. And they brought him home.

But there was one sad story. The guy who was in law school that committed suicide on my watch. Adam.

Young guy. Always looked like a deer in the headlights. Had no interest in law. Came from a lineage of lawyers, and was forced into law school. That had a lot to do with his troubled state of mind. But that wasn't considered. All they were looking for were biochemical imbalances as reasons for his insanity. Medicate the shit out of him, etc. His wife really wanted him to be a lawyer. She was giving him the same pressure.

I really liked him. I related to him, because I myself was thinking about law school. Medical school, even becoming a massage therapist. Law school. I was thinking about everything. Private detective. But mostly law school.

He trusted me, for good reason. I was resonating with him. Took him for walks outside. One time, I actually took him to his apartment, on the subway to get some books.

He kept saying, "This psychiatrist doesn't understand me at all".

If you're a private patient out in the world and you don't get along with your psychiatrist, you can go find another one.

But in the hospital, there's some arbitrary way they determine what psychiatrist you get. It wasn't based on who's the best for you. And I agreed with Adam. His psychiatrist was the wrong guy.

They gave him pharmaceuticals, forcibly. Once you give someone enough pharmaceuticals forcibly, they become lethargic. You never have to force them again.

So, he became very quiet, until one day he got a butter knife from his lunch and threatened his psychiatrist. And then he was put on continuous observation.

Up until then, there were no signs of violence. None. And this was an "aha" moment for the psychiatrist. Aha, he really is insane, you see?

And it was an aha moment for me. I just went "Aha, he's been driven to this."

After that, he was not only overmedicated, but he was given ECT (Electroconvulsive Therapy).

But still, he escaped. And he jumped in front of a subway car.

I grieved for a long time. I still grieve for him. I felt responsible, I thought maybe I didn't go far enough, maybe I didn't... whatever.

That was the only suicide on my watch. I shouldn't be saying "only". There should be no suicides on anybody's watch.

I should have gone further. I thought he needed a different therapist. I did talk to his resident. I didn't talk to the resident's boss. I should have.

Patients

One guy came in. A young Portuguese guy. His name was Jesu, which is Jesus.

He was a hitch-hiker who had been thrown out of a moving car. And he came in clutching a Bible that was all tied up with rope. He wouldn't let it go.

I saw it was the Bible and said, "Jesu? Why is the Bible all tied up in rope?" And he said, "I've trapped the devil."

He was a wonderful guy. I liked his attitude. Somebody had to trap that damn devil.

Then there was this Italian guy. His name was Antonio. He was older, 55. He and I became friends. He was southern Italian, Calabrese. His language was very close to Sicilian. We could talk to each other.

He told everyone that his cousin was screwing his wife. And he was vivid in describing how this cousin was screwing her, giving the times and places and even sexual positions.

He was so convincing, everyone was considering the possibility that maybe he's not that psychotic. Maybe his cousin really is screwing his wife.

His wife came in to visit. She was a modest, respectable 55-year-old Italian woman. I had a visit with her without the husband. In Italian. And it was all rather embarrassing for both of us. She knew very well what was happening.

And she said, "Oh, he's convincing, yes. Maybe you believe him. *Forse, tu cicrede.* Maybe you think that his cousin and I..."

I said, "*Signora, e possibile, no?*"

And she said, "*Non e possibile.* It's not possible."

I said, "No?"

She said, "His cousin has been dead fifteen years."

I said, "Fifteen years? That long?"

She said, "*Quindici anni.*"

And then she said, "Tella da *dottore.*"

I said, "I'll tell the doctor."

He was treated, and discharged. His wife came to get him, and she gave me a bottle of delicious homemade wine. My job had some benefits.

I liked to take patients out for walks. Sometimes when you're not allowed to. They're supposed to be signed out by a nurse, and I wasn't a nurse, I didn't have the authority.

I'd say, "I don't give a shit. I'm taking them out. and I'm going to come back with them too." I'd say to the patients, "Come on, you have to finish your desert. Everybody get your coats on."

They got their coats on and we'd take a walk through the Kensington Market. Eight patients, 7:30 at night, in winter, it's dark, lots of activity. The stalls are being dismantled. I'm not even behind them. They're all behind me. Except for the ones that are around me. I'm not watching to see who's going to escape. And some of them were committed!

I acted from the heart, and I trusted them. I said, "If you don't come back, you're going to break my heart. And you're going to piss me off, but mostly I'll be upset."

I didn't have to tell them outright not to escape. They knew, it's Charly taking us for a walk when he's not supposed to. Again. They always came back with me. And the nurses were waiting, wagging their fingers at me.

One Sunday morning, I was assigned to the Clinical Investigation Unit, CIU. All the anorexics and the bulimics ended up there. Sixteen-year-old girls mostly. It's the nature of the pathology.

I say, "Come on. We're going for a walk."

I took them to the Chinese Bakery on Baldwin Street. It's the only place open on Sunday morning. There's a little park nearby. We're sitting there.

I say, "Please wait here."

I buy all kinds of tarts, custard tarts and lemon tarts and cookies. I bring them out, and I say, "Come on! Eat!" I was an Italian mother! I say, "Eat! What's the matter with you? Look at you! You're damn tooth picks! All of you!"

They say "Charly, we're sick."

I say, "Sick? You're sick because you're not eating! You're not getting any food! Try some of these tarts!"

They would pick at the crust and hand it back to me. Nobody ate. But that was me: thump therapy. Mr. Thump Therapy.

I believed in reality testing. Everybody handled patients with kid leather gloves, but I was into being real. They called me the "thump therapist". I acted like a Hamiltonian: "What the fuck do you think you're doing, man? The television isn't talking just to you! It's talking to millions of people!"

I'm not saying it worked.

Late at night, I was doing continuous observation with a suicidal patient who's being obnoxious. We're watching TV, and I'm putting my feet on a footstool. Just when I'd get relaxed, he kicks the footstool away.

Just the two of us in the room. Every time I went to put my feet up, he'd kick the footstool away. He'd go, "Heh, heh, heh."

I thought, "You bastard".

I get out of my chair. He's standing up, going, "Heh, heh, heh."

Quietly, I go behind him. He thinks I'm leaving. He starts to sit down. I pull the chair away.

Thump. Right on his ass.

I'm his primary therapist, and therapists are not supposed to do stuff like that. But again, I'm the thump therapist.

After that, we had a nice time watching TV and chatting.

A Minstrel's Tune

Reality testing, aka thump therapy, was not my only idea of how to run a psychiatric hospital. I had two other ideas.

Number one, they need a massage therapist here. Because no one touches psychiatric patients. They were like lepers. I actually put a written request in. Bring in a massage therapist, and let these people be touched once in a while. That was the request I made in writing to my director. She just grinned. I thought these people would get well if you just touch them once in a while.

Number two idea, I thought, a piano! We need a piano!

This was the Inn on the Clarke. They only accepted sophisticated patients, educated, articulate. And they all seemed to have musical ability. Maybe because they grew up well-off and had lessons on piano, or whatever. Some of them played the guitar. There were flautists. There seemed to be an affinity between psychosis and music. Art in general.

I'd bring my harmonica and start jamming when they brought instruments in, but the instrument that was lacking was the piano. The guys had piano lessons. The women had piano lessons. But there was no piano. I asked, and the response was, "We have no funds for a piano."

"Well, maybe we can get some funds. How about a fundraiser? I'll organize a variety show, and we'll raise money to buy a piano."

They were amused.

"Sure", I said. "The fundraiser will be in the Grand Rounds auditorium."

It held three hundred people. And it's not used for anything but Grand Rounds. Apparently, there was no protocol that allowed us to use the Grand Rounds auditorium for entertainment. So, my request was ignored.

I was in the line-up at the bank across the street from the Clarke, waiting to withdraw some cash.

Dr. Rakoff, the god, the man who picked me up on the highway to Hamilton, came and stood behind me.

I was an incessant songwriter. Since he was behind me, he heard me singing to myself, as I was writing:

>*Revel in your melancholy*
>*Sink into your sadness.*

Just then, he taps me on the shoulder, and says, "Young man. Charly."

I say, "Oh, hi Dr. Rakoff."

He says, "So, what are you doing now?"

"I'm writing a song."

He says, "Might I be privy to your song?"

I say, "Well, it's not finished. But so far, it goes…"

>*Revel in your melancholy*
>*Sink into your sadness*
>*Hearty laughter won't seem folly*
>*Nor will downright madness.*

He says, "Hearty laughter won't seem folly? Nor will downright madness?"

I say, "Yes."

He says "Yes. Yes indeed."

When I went back to the Clarke the next day, I was called into the office. "Charly, about that variety show."

"Ah, never mind."

"You can have the Grand Rounds auditorium. Check the schedule and reserve it."

"What happened?"

"Let's see what you can do."

I say, "Thank you." Then I think, "Now what?" I'm on the hook. I said I could organize a variety show. But the truth was, I'd never done anything like that before. And now, holy shit, I've got to do it!

So, I put up some posters asking people to perform. Patients, doctors, nurses, psych assistants. Anyone. I thought of a name: *Escape Hatch 11*. Because we were on the eleventh floor, and the variety show would be an escape hatch to another world. For all of us. And I waited for people to sign up.

So... nobody signed up. It was three weeks to the big day. Nobody. I checked. I said, "Have I still got the auditorium booked?"

And they said, "Well, yes."

I said, "Well, the show must go on. If I have to tap dance, sing and play the harmonica, the show's going to go on."

A Simple Minstrel's Tune

A simple minstrel's tune
Brings gladness, maybe gloom
Go on and take a chance
Be daring when you dance.

The wizard longs to teach
There's rainbows within reach
And children wise and bold
Seek treasures beyond gold.

Revel in your melancholy
Sink into your sadness
Hearty laughter won't seem folly
Nor will downright madness.

Life is but a dream
We're puppets in a scene
The world is just a stage
Take a bow, and turn the page.

Revel in your melancholy
Sink into your sadness
Hearty laughter won't seem folly
Nor will downright madness.

Charly's Piano
Act II

Have a Good Time

Preach like Peter, pray like Paul,
Even saints gotta have a ball,

Have a good time,
Have a good time,
Have a good time,
Rock and roll all night long.

Spend your money, dance and shout,
Get up, get down, let it all hang out,

Have a good time,
Have a good time,
Have a good time,
Rock and roll all night long.

Sun goes down, work day's done,
Spread your wings, have yourself some fun,

Have a good time,
Have a good time,
Have a good time,
And rock and roll all night
Have a good time,
And rock and roll all night
Have a good time,
And rock and roll all night long.

The Cat Woman

I was doing rounds at night, full moon. I loved doing rounds on a full moon. Nobody is sleeping in a psychiatric hospital on a full moon night.

It was 3 am. Beatrice, the cat woman, was in her room, painting with watercolour. I watched her dip her brush, touch it to a colour, and then carefully stroke the paper. I said, "May I see take a closer look?"

She nodded. There were plants intertwining, filling the page. But, instead of flowers on the plants, there were faces. Most of the faces were fellow psychiatric patients. And her own face peeked out from many plants.

I said, "This is very interesting. I love it".

And she said, "If you can guess what the title is, I'll give it to you. After it dries."

I said, "Paradise?"

She said, "It's yours. Tomorrow morning, it'll be dry, and you can have it." And it's hanging on my wall to this day.

The next day, I came to pick up the painting. And she said, "This show you're organizing?"

I said, "Nobody is signing up. I may have to do it all myself. But it's going to go on."

And she said, "I'll sing a song."

I said, "What song?"

She said, "It's a song I wrote."

I said, "What's it about?"

She said. "It's about what happens when you lose everything. It's called 'When the well runs dry'."

I said, "Yeah, that'll be great."

And then, magically, there was this trickle of patients. And then there was a trickle of nurses. And then there was a trickle of residents, psychiatrists. And then all the Filipino and Jamaican nurses said they would cook, serve food, and sell food for audience members to bring home for their supper.

And I couldn't believe what was happening. Writers, musicians, the newspaper editor (all patients), started writing. They wrote skits for the psychiatrists, skits for the patients. And the patients wrote skits for themselves.

Something was happening beyond me. I felt like, when the bullseye gets big... I was only this little dot, and suddenly... I was a little dot, surrounded by this wonderful thing, this energy. And I was the MC, see? I was the dot.

They closed the Clarke the afternoon of the concert. Everyone wanted to see the show. The auditorium was packed, 300 people. Admission was on a sliding scale. And donations were accepted. The food was laid out, and everyone was buying food to eat and to take home. My fellow psych assistants put some finishing touches on a Christmas tree that adorned the stage.

I looked out at the auditorium as everyone was coming in, filling all the seats. As the MC, it was up to me to start the show.

I was on one side of the stage. On the other side was Beatrice. She was the first act, because she wanted to get it over with. She was poised like a sprinter. And from the other side of the stage, I looked at her. She looked at me in panic, and she was like, "Get me on now, Charly! Because I'm on the brink of leaving."

And it never occurred to me that she has a right to be nervous. I should escort her off. She's a psychiatric patient! I just thought, "The show must go on!" There were three hundred people out there! She was twenty years old, she was just a young girl. But I didn't think of it that way. The show must go on!

And she didn't run away. I crossed the stage, and I took her hand and brought her to centre stage, and she said, "Well, stand behind me." And I introduced her.

And I just stood behind her with my harmonica. And she did this demure, but gut-wrenching rendition of her song.

Song: When the Well Runs Dry

Whatcha gonna do when the well runs dry?
And you find there really ain't no pie in the sky,

Whatcha gonna do?
How ya gonna make yourself high
When the well runs dry?

You can't buy bread with pocket lint,
You can't manufacture money if you don't own a mint,

Wear them rags
And learn what not to buy,
When the well runs dry.

When the well runs dry,
And there's no more tears to cry,
You can't even afford to die
When the well runs dry
When the well runs dry.

Ain't no easy street without a job,
The neighbourhood so poor, nobody left to rob.

Shake your pride
Ain't nothin' you won't try,
When the well runs dry.

When the well runs dry,
And there's no more tears to cry,
You can't even afford to die
When the well runs dry
When the well runs dry.

When the well runs dry
When the well runs dry.

The concert

The actual concert was made up of skits, stand up, songs and a dancer. One of the patients was a jazz dancer.

I wrote this song, "Pills They Keep Popping into Me", to the tune of "Raindrops Keep Falling on My Head".

And this woman, Rosemary, had never performed in her life. She was your typical rich Rosedale woman. I don't even think she was insane. The Clarke was the place where, when husbands got sick of their wives, they declared them insane, and put them in there, and they should have sent them to Florida, or something. But they came to the Clarke. And they weren't always unhappy about being at the Clarke.

So, I had her singing this song, and she was holding a paper bag. And her analyst, Doctor Miller, was there. So were Doctor Rakoff and Doctor Persaud. They were all sitting in the front row.

Pills They Keep Popping into Me

> *Pills they keep popping into me,*
> *But that is the thing they do here in psychiatry,*
> *There's no way I can flee,*
> *Those pills they keep popping into me,*
> *They keep popping.*
>
> *So, I just did me some talking to myself*
> *Said, "Self, I've got to find a way right back into health*
> *beyond Chlorpromazine."*
> *Those pills they keep popping into me,*
> *They keep popping.*
>
> *But there's one thing*
> *I know*
> *Those pills in here to treat me*
> *Won't defeat me,*
> *It won't be long 'till happiness*
> *Comes out to greet me.*
> *Greet me,*
> *Greet me.*

Pills, they keep popping into me,
They say it's the way to get me back to sanity,
When will I be free?
Of pills they keep popping into me,
They keep popping.

Please let me be.
I just wanna be me.
Please let me be.
I just wanna be free.

And she reached into her bag, and she pulled out handfuls of multi-coloured jelly beans, and tossed them onto the laps of the psychiatrists in the front row.

They were shocked. They didn't expect her to be on stage. This is a lady who dressed with white gloves up to her elbows. And they didn't expect to be lampooned that way by a patient who gave no indication that she was the lampooning type. They were taken aback. But they were smiling.

The whole evening was like that. Psychiatrists acting like patients, and patients acting like psychiatrists.

One of the skits was written by one of the newspaper reporters, a patient. One patient played a psychiatrist. And a patient comes in (who was a real patient), and they did this scene, the one patient acting just like a real psychiatrist. Well, why not? He knew what a psychiatrist acts like. And the other patient had no trouble acting like a psychotic patient, because he was psychotic patient!

After the fake therapy session, the psychiatrist said, "Okay, your next appointment will be..." and he wrote down the next appointment and the patient left. The doctor got up. He put on his hat and coat, took a banana out of his pocket, scratched his armpits and hopped off the stage.

Standing ovation.

We closed the concert by putting lyrics up on the screen and getting everyone to sing Christmas songs.

And the whole audience— patients, doctors, nurses, psych assistants— sang Christmas songs together.

The Duchess

And a lot of money was made. Enough to buy a piano.

How do you buy a piano? I hadn't thought about that. I don't play piano.

The most psychotic patient there was a woman who had recently been admitted. She thought she was the Duchess de Rothschild.

She had checked into Royal York Hotel. After two weeks, they realized that The Duchess was a psychotic woman who couldn't pay her bills. So, to the Clarke she came, and I became her primary counsellor.

She was tall, statuesque, well dressed. She wore jewellery. Costume jewellery. She looked a little odd, but not that odd for the times "that are a-changing".

Her delusion was so fixed that the nurses all called her Duchess. Why argue? But I wouldn't call her Duchess. Her name was Mary. Thump therapy. I called her Mary, and she accepted it.

I learned that she was a figure skater, at some point in her life. And I had a suspicion that she was a piano player. She had all the earmarks of it. Especially her hands. That's what my intuition told me.

And I said, "Have you ever had piano lessons?"

She said, "Certainly. In my younger days, I was quite an accomplished pianist. Amateur, of course."

I said, "I'm going to buy a piano. I need you to tell me if it's any good."

She said, "I would be happy to oblige."

So, I phoned the number in the ad, and got the address. They told me where it was. Of course, they assumed I was driving, but I didn't have a car. I had to figure out how to get there by public transit.

So, I found someone to sign out The Duchess, and we walked to the subway. We made quite an impression getting in the subway car, this bearded hippie and this haughty lady, dressed for evening in the middle of the afternoon. As the Duchess stood proudly in her fake fur coat and a muff to keep her hands warm.

From the subway, we transferred to a bus. It didn't go all the way, though. We got off at the end of the line. What to do now?

We could call the piano owner for instructions or assistance, but there was no phone booth in sight. Just a snow-covered road stretching toward the horizon.

Well, I did what I would do, Duchess or no Duchess. I stuck my thumb out.

After a few minutes, a car pulled over. I got into the front seat, and the Duchess climbed into the back. She was being a good sport about it. That was a relief.

And then we took another bus, and we got to a gas station. And I said, "I'm trying to get to here." Pointing at a map.

And there was nothing but a gravel road. And they said, "You're trying to get to the so-and-so residence". And they let me use the telephone.

I called, and a voice said, "Yes, hello. How can I help you?"

I said, "It's me, the guy who's buying the piano. The person I'm with and I came by public transportation. We don't have the means. . ."

"Oh! So sorry. There'll be a car there for you in ten minutes."

So, the Duchess and I, Mary, are waiting for the car, and a black stretch limo arrives, with a chauffeur, wearing a hat. And he gets out of the car, and he opens the door and Mary goes in, and she gives me this *look*.

I get in. We're in a stretch limo, me and The Duchess, and lo and behold, it's this fabulous estate, beautifully decorated for Christmas, and we go in.

I had never been in any place like this. I grew up on Park Street, in Hamilton. This place—huge rooms, mahogany, plate glass window looking out on a terraced garden, marble coffee table. Crystal chandelier. And the biggest Christmas tree I'd ever seen, for indoors.

The Duchess casts her eye over the décor, nods in approval, and moves graciously toward the gentleman who had come to the door. I move in quickly, before The Duchess introduces herself and starts dropping anecdotes about the Rothschilds.

"I'm Charly. We've come about the piano."

He barely seems to glance at us. "Oh, yes, yes, yes. The piano's over there, it's over there. It's in pretty good shape, but you have to expect to tune it when its delivered. But, it's really quite tuned up. We're getting a grand, you know."

The Duchess said, "A grand, yes. So much more satisfactory. When I was a girl..."

I intervened. I said, "Do you mind if my friend..."

The man said, "Go ahead."

The Duchess sat on the bench, straight-backed, and touched the keys with her long delicate fingers. She started to play. She played for about two minutes. She said, "It's all right."

And I thought, "Okay." I said, "It's all right. Here's the money for the piano." The asking price. I pulled a wad of bills out of the pocket of my jeans.

He said, "Okay. Where is it going, by the way?"

And I said, "The Clarke Institute of Psychiatry."

He took a second look at both of us. I'm sure he thought, "There is something very strange going on here." He said, "Well, are you going send somebody to pick it up?"

I thought, "Oh yeah, delivery." I said, "Yeah, yeah." I said, "Maybe I'll get somebody with a pickup truck."

He said, "Usually professional movers of pianos would move a piano."

And I said, "We haven't got any money for that."

He looked at me. Then he looked at The Duchess. And the Duchess looked at him, as if from a great height. He said, "Just tell me the date that you want it delivered. I'll deliver it for you."

I said, "Okay."

And he said, "Upon delivery, it's going to get out of tune."

The Duchess's look didn't waver. He said, "I'll have somebody tune it for you too."

I said, "Thanks."

And the Duchess smiled sweetly. Nodded. Then she looked at me. And winked.

He drove us back to the gas station, and the gas station people worked out a route where we didn't have to hitch hike.

And lo and behold, three days later, the piano was delivered. And a piano tuner arrived and tuned it. The piano was installed in our lounge on the eleventh floor. And, of course, the first person to sit down and play it was: The Duchess.

With her regal air, she seated herself on the bench, waited a moment to heighten the expectation, and launched into "Fur Elise". There was applause. She nodded her thanks, and said: "I had a very good teacher, as a child. My father, the Duke de Rothschild, loved music."

She often played the piano, and it probably helped her make the transition to regular life.

Years later, a poem was published in *Phoenix Rising*, a magazine by and for ex-inmates of the Clarke. It included the lines:

"I was down with the frets
sitting on that doggasted sofa
in the Lost Duchess Lounge
it's named after a local legend..."

Yes indeed. The Lost Duchess Lounge.

Back to the Clarke

I left the Clarke and finished my university. Became a social
worker. Got married. Years passed. Now I was a mental health and
addictions consultant in Kingston. Fourteen years since I had been
to the Clarke Institute.

I happened to be in Toronto with my daughter Selina, who was
eight. We were on Harbord Street, near where I had lived. I don't
remember what we were doing there, or why it was just Selina and
me.

I said, "Let's go visit the Clarke."

She said, "Why?"

I said, "I don't know. I used to work there. I'd like to see it again."

She said, "Okay, Dad." She was eight, and very self-assured.

So, we went to the eleventh floor. There were barriers in front of
the elevators. Barriers and barrenness. It was like a place that was
once a gold mining town, and was now a ghost town. There were
no staff to be seen.

I didn't see any patients, either. There was no one milling around.
it was incredibly different.

A security guard came and asked, "What do you want?"

I said, "I used to work here." I said, "I'm trying to find out who's
still here."

I asked, "Is Senna working here? Senna, is she here?"

The security guard said, "Senna?"

"Okay. Is Dr. Persaud here? Dr. Rakoff?"

"Dr. Rakoff has an office, but he doesn't really work here. He's
retired."

I said, "Can I see him?"

And he said, "He's not in right now."

"Ahh."

"All right. Ausa? Is she here?"

"Ausa's here. Okay. I'll get her."

And I'm standing with Selina, and from a distance I see this white-haired Filipino woman, and she looks at me... and I had grey hair and I didn't have the beard, and we looked at each other from a distance. It was almost like there was... if I was doing it in a movie, there'd be smoke between us. And she approached me, and she opened the door, and she said, "Charly!"

We hugged.

I said "Ausa, what happened?"

She said, "It's not the Clarke that you knew. Patients aren't like they used to be. And staff isn't like it used to be. This is not the Clarke, that you're visiting. They call it CAMH. This is the new reality. Over-medication..."

I said, "Ausa, they over-medicated patients back then."

She says, "Oh no. Oh no. It's completely changed. It's *way* over-medication. And they don't have a rehabilitation component. Nobody even plays cards with them anymore."

And then she said, "But I want to show you something."

I didn't know where she was taking me. And we arrived at the piano, that looked like it hadn't been played in ten years.

And she looked at Selina, and she said, "This is your daddy's piano." She said, "Your dad put this piano here."

And she asked, "Do you play piano?"

Selina said "Yes, I play piano."

And Ausa opened the piano, and Selina played.

Ausa and I went to talk. And in the background, we heard Selina playing this out of tune piano.

And I realized that... times change. They don't treat people like they used to.

Something About Toronto (3)

Christmas in Toronto,
Shops and decorations
Hanging onto friendships
Party invitations
Snowy cold Decembers
Memories fly like embers
How I loved Toronto town.

CN Tower looming,
A beacon for the lost souls,
Caffeine morning grooming
Slipping into work clothes,
Things forever changing
Skyline rearranging
Farewell to Toronto town.

Living a crazy wild city scene
Subways street cars College and Queen
It's not Paris New York or Rome
But it was home
My Toronto home
But it was home
My Toronto home
My Toronto Home.

Something 'bout Toronto
Fills me full of wonder
Something 'bout Toronto
Makes me buckle under
Was it luck that brought me
Or did I come by blunder?
Something 'bout Toronto town.

Something 'bout Toronto town.

www.ingramcontent.com/pod-product-compliance
Lightning Source LLC
Chambersburg PA
CBHW021915040426
42447CB00007B/870